DISCOVER AND DO!

HISTORY

ROMANS

Written by Jane Lacey

Enslow PUBLISHING

Published in 2024 by Enslow Publishing, LLC
2544 Clinton Street
Buffalo, NY 14224

Editor: Katie Dicker
Designer: Clare Nicholas
Series designer: Rocket Design (East Anglia) Ltd

Manufactured in the United States of America

CPSIA compliance information: Batch #CW24ENS: For further information contact
Enslow Publishing LLC, New York, New York at 1-800-398-2504.

Please visit our website, www.enslowpublishing.com. For a free color catalog of all our high-quality books,
call toll free 1-800-398-2504 or fax 1-877-980-4454.

Cataloging-in-Publication Data

Names: Lacey, Jane.
Title: Romans / Jane Lacey.
Description: New York : Enslow Publishing, 2024. | Series: Discover and do: history | Includes glossary and index.
Identifiers: ISBN 9781978538290 (pbk.) | ISBN 9781978538306 (library bound) | ISBN 9781978538313 (ebook)
Subjects: LCSH: Rome--Civilization--Juvenile literature.
Classification: LCC DG77.L33 2024 | DDC 937--dc23

Picture credits:
t=top b=bottom m=middle l=left r=right

Shutterstock: Bahau cover/title page l and 10b, Kundra cover/title page r, Nikola Knezevic 4 and 20b, Macrovector 5tl, 6b,12b and 29b, StockSmartStart 5tr and 25t, GoodStudio 5br, 22b, 26b and 31b, JeniFoto 7t and 32, Peter Hermes Furian 7b, Gilmanshin 8t and 23t, Sentavio 8b, Yaroslaff 9t, Siberian Art 10t and 30b, D.R.3D 11t, BlueRingMedia 13t, Prostock-studio 13b, JethroT 14t, Piranhi 15t, karnavalfoto 16t, steve estvanik 16b, Giamka 18t, A-R-T 18bl, BlackMac 18b, YUCALORA 20t, 29t and 30t, emperorcosar 24t, Malchev 26t and 31m, delcarmat 27t, 28 and 31t; iStock: Bakhauaddin-bek Sopybekov 4 and 20b, wjarek 6t, ZU_09 12t, Khosrork 17b, Keith Lance 21t, clu 24b; Alamy: Album 17t, © Museum of London/Heritage-Images 22t; Getty: Luigi Galante 14b.

All design elements from Shutterstock.
Craft models from a previous series made by Anna-Marie D'Cruz/photos by Steve Shott.

DISCOVER AND DO!

HISTORY

ROMANS

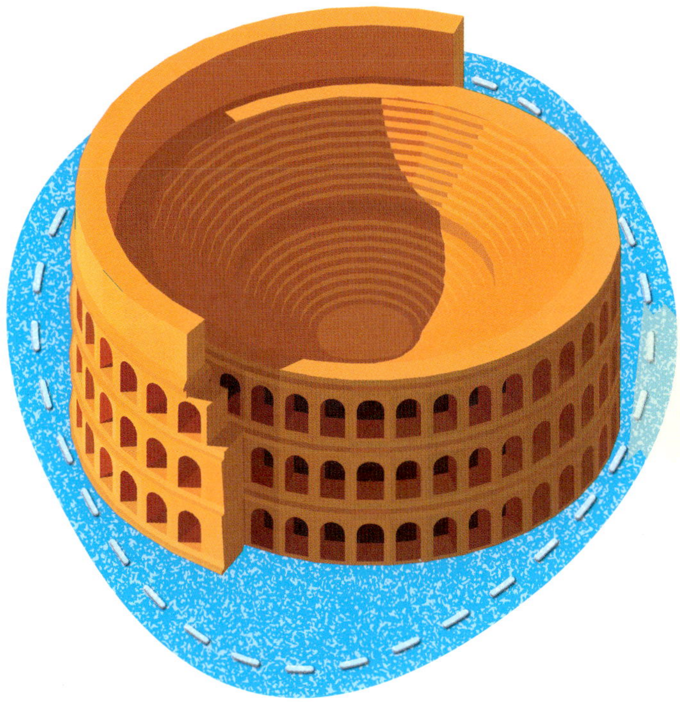

Written by Jane Lacey

Enslow PUBLISHING

CONTENTS

Words that appear in **bold** can be found in the glossary on pages 28–29.

THE ROMANS

The Romans were the people of the city of Rome. They built a powerful empire that lasted for around 500 years from 27 BCE to 476 CE. According to legend, Rome was built in 753 BCE by twin brothers Romulus and Remus who were brought up by a mother wolf.

Rome was named after Romulus.

Ancient Rome

The city of Rome became very powerful with grand government buildings, temples, bath houses, theaters, and statues. Today, Rome is the capital city of Italy. The remains of ancient Roman buildings can still be seen there.

Roads, bridges, and ships

The Romans were clever **engineers**. They built thousands of miles of roads with bridges over rivers and valleys, and ships that sailed the Mediterranean Sea. Roads and ships allowed the Romans to travel quickly and **conquer** surrounding countries.

The Colosseum, where Romans watched **gladiators** fight, still stands in Rome today.

Huge empire

With the help of a powerful army, the Roman Empire grew rapidly. At the height of its power, it spread across North Africa right through Europe to faraway Britain.

The areas in red show the countries in the Roman Empire.

ROMAN EMPERORS

At first, Rome was ruled by kings and then by an elected senate. However, as the city's power grew, senators and army generals fought to control Roman lands. Eventually one person took over, the emperor.

a statue of Augustus Caesar, the first emperor

The first emperor

Many people thought the famous Roman general, Julius Caesar, would be the first Roman emperor. But he was murdered. A few years later, in 27 BCE, his nephew, Augustus Caesar, became the first of 49 emperors.

Emperor god

Roman emperors were very powerful. The emperor's head was stamped on Roman coins. Emperors were worshipped like gods. Temples were built to them all over the Empire.

These Roman coins show the head of Emperor Trajan who ruled from 98 CE.

ACTIVITY

MAKE A LAUREL WREATH

Emperors were not kings and they did not wear crowns. They wore wreaths made from laurel to celebrate victory and power.

You will need:

- **dark green construction paper**
- **scissors**
- **pencil**
- **glue or tape**

1. Cut out a band of dark green paper about 1.5 inches (4 cm) wide to fit around your head.

2. Cut out about 20 leaf shapes from more green paper. Stick the leaves onto the band so that they overlap.

3. Glue the ends of the band together. Put on your wreath and become a Roman emperor!

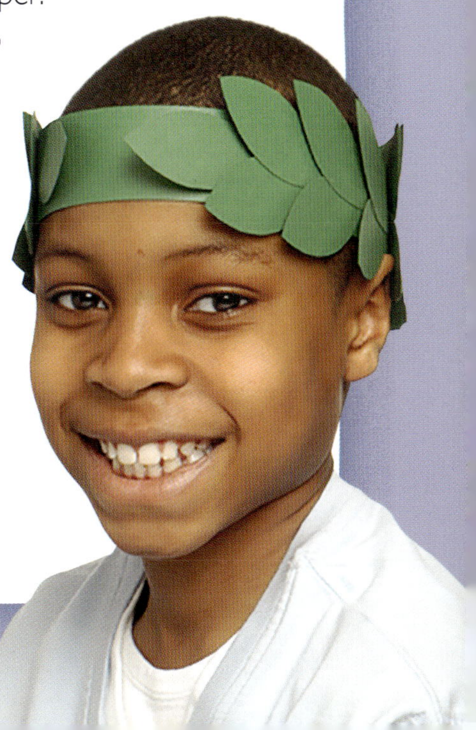

THE ARMY

The Roman Empire needed a large army to conquer and control the lands they invaded. The army was important to the emperor, and he made sure his soldiers were looked after.

A soldier's life

A soldier joined the army for 25 years. He was paid in money and in salt. During a war, soldiers marched many miles a day, wearing leather sandals and carrying heavy equipment. They built roads and bridges as they went, setting up camp each night.

Soldiers used a stabbing sword and a spear and had metal armor to protect them.

The Roman army was highly trained. Only men were allowed to be soldiers.

Legion

A **legion** was made up of about 5,000 soldiers called legionaries. They were organized into smaller groups of about 100 soldiers called **centuries**, led by an officer called a centurion. Each legion carried an eagle **standard**, which was the symbol of its power.

If a standard was captured by the enemy, the legion broke up.

ACTIVITY

MAKE AN EAGLE STANDARD

You will need:

- **card stock**
- **pencil**
- **scissors**
- **two wrapping paper tubes**
- **silver paint**
- **two red ribbons**
- **glue or tape**

1. Copy the shapes below onto card stock. You will need three of the circle shape. Make the eagle as big as this page.

2. Using two tubes from rolls of wrapping paper, squash the end of one inside the other.

3. Paint the shapes and tubes with silver paint. Let those dry.

4. Stick the painted shapes onto the pole with the eagle at the top.

5. Decorate with red ribbons to complete the standard.

LIFE IN ROMAN TIMES

Everyone had their place in Roman times. Citizens were men who had been born in Rome or had served Rome in a war. Non-citizens were born outside Rome. Enslaved people had no rights and belonged to their owner.

This Roman carving shows mother, father, and son. The boy is dressed like his father.

Roman families

The father was the head of a Roman family. He was expected to look after his wife and children, and their enslaved people. Girls were expected to grow up to be wives and mothers. The women managed the household and the family money. Families sometimes took in and looked after someone who had no family.

Enslaved people were not paid.

Life as an enslaved person

An enslaved person was either born into enslavement or was a captive of war. They worked hard in the household or on farms or building sites. Enslaved people were often badly treated, but some owners tried to make them feel part of the family.

Jobs to do

- fetch water
- clean
- shop
- tend the fire
- cook
- serve meals
- help the women to dress and do their hair
- look after the children

ACTIVITY

DAY AS AN ENSLAVED PERSON

You will need:

- **paper**
- **pencil and pens**

1. Imagine you are enslaved in Roman times. Who owns you? How do they treat you?
2. Write about the daily life of someone who is enslaved.
3. Draw a picture of yourself at work.

Today, important guests are coming to dinner. I'll be in trouble if anything goes wrong!

HOUSES

A Roman country house was called a villa. A town house was called a domus. A family would live in one part of a house, their enslaved people in the other.

In crowded towns, people lived in four- or five-story apartment blocks called **insulae**, as shown by this ruin.

Villas

Remains of Roman villas have been found all over the Roman Empire. They belonged to rich farmers and landowners. They had many rooms, which were richly decorated with wall paintings and statues. Roman houses often had a shady courtyard with a pool to collect rainwater.

Can you identify the different rooms of this Roman villa?

Mosaics

Some villas had mosaics. These were pictures and patterns made of small pieces of stone or tiles. The pictures often told stories of gods and goddesses.

This mosaic of Venus, the goddess of love, was found in a Roman villa in the United Kingdom.

ACTIVITY

MAKE A ROMAN MOSAIC

You will need:

- **pencil**
- **colored paper**
- **scissors**
- **glue**

1. Copy this outline of a Roman mosaic.
2. Cut out squares from different-colored pieces of paper.
3. Paint one section of your picture at a time with glue.
4. Fill each section with colored squares.

CHILDHOOD

The children of enslaved and poor people did not go to school. They had to work as soon as they were big enough. In richer families, boys went to school or were taught at home. Girls were sometimes taught to read and write.

Child's play

Some Roman children had dolls and toy animals to play with; they flew kites and played on swings and seesaws. Children played board games or other simple games, such as marbles.

Knucklebones was a game like modern jacks.

This mosaic shows young children herding geese as part of their work.

Growing up

When a new baby was born, it was put at its father's feet. If he accepted the baby, it became part of the family. Children learned to be like their parents. Often, children were given a charm called a bulla to protect them. Boys became adults at 14 and girls when they married at 13 or 14.

Children kept their bulla in a bag, which they wore as a bracelet or necklace.

ACTIVITY

MAKE A BULLA

You will need:

- **air-drying clay**
- **small square of cloth**
- **colored string**

1. Think of something that is special to you. It must be something you can model out of clay to be your secret charm.

2. Form a clay model of the item and leave it to dry.
3. Put your charm in a small square of cloth.
4. Tie the ends of the square with colored string and hang it around your wrist.

LETTERS AND NUMBERS

Latin was spoken in Ancient Rome. We call Latin a dead language because today no groups speak it in daily conversation. Many modern languages, including English, are written in the same alphabet the Romans used.

This replica of a wax tablet shows how it was used.

Scrolls

The Romans wrote on rolls of **papyrus** called scrolls with pen and ink. Children practiced writing on wax tablets. They scored letters and numbers with a pointed stylus. The wax could be scraped off to use again.

Roman **numerals** were seven letters. The year 1576 would be written MDLXXVI.

I	→ 1
V	→ 5
X	→ 10
L	→ 50
C	→ 100
D	→ 500
M	→ 1000

Choose the font TIMES NEW ROMAN on a computer and type some words in capital letters. Compare them to this Roman inscription.

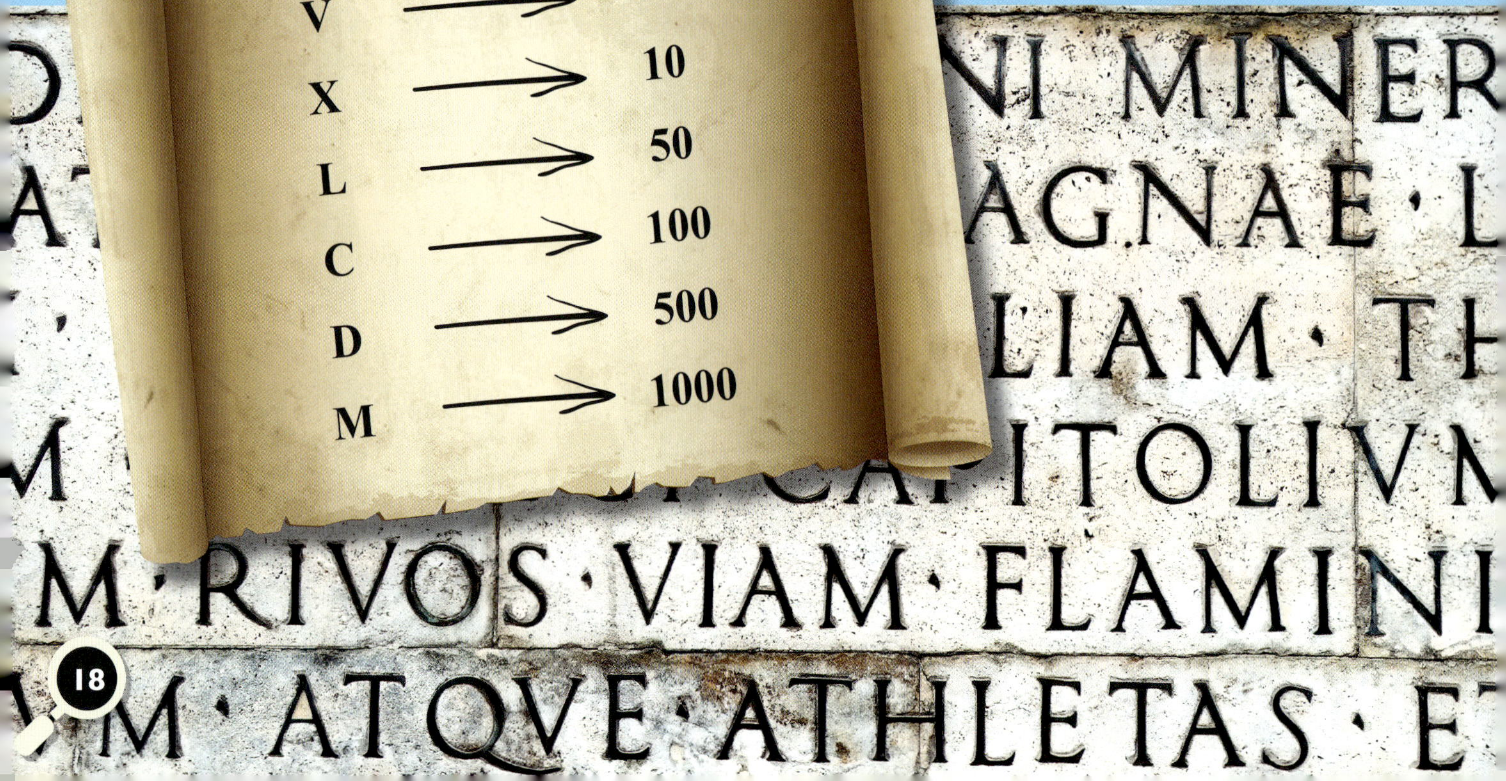

ACTIVITY

MAKE A WAX TABLET

You will need:

- **candle**
- **black and brown card stock**
- **scissors**
- **glue**
- **pencil**

1. Rub the end of a candle on a piece of black card stock to make a layer of wax.

2. Cut out a frame of brown card stock and stick it onto the black card stock.

3. Use a pencil to score Roman letters and numerals into the wax.

4. When the wax is covered in writing, smooth it with a piece of card stock.

5. Rub on a new layer of wax and use the tablet again.

ENTERTAINMENT

The Romans celebrated many religious festivals with entertainment. There were three main kinds of entertainment: plays, games, and races. These were each held in a specially designed building.

Theater

Roman theaters could hold thousands of people. Actors were popular stars, just like they are today. The plays were comedies, to make people laugh, or serious tragedies.

Actors wore masks so their expressions could be seen from the back seats.

Games

Roman games were bloody and deadly. They were held in huge **amphitheaters**, like the Colosseum, where crowds gathered to watch gladiator fights and reenactments of wars.

Gladiators were criminals, war captives, or enslaved people. Some were professional fighters.

Chariot races

Chariot races were held in an arena called the circus (or **hippodrome**). Chariots pulled by two or four horses raced around a track. Teams of racers had their own supporters, like football teams have today.

Some chariot races had around 250,000 supporters cheering on their team.

ACTIVITY

MAKE A MODEL CHARIOT

You will need:

- **gold card stock**
- **pencil**
- **scissors**
- **modeling tool**
- **glue**

1. Copy the shapes below onto gold card stock and cut them out. Score a pattern onto the side with a modeling tool.

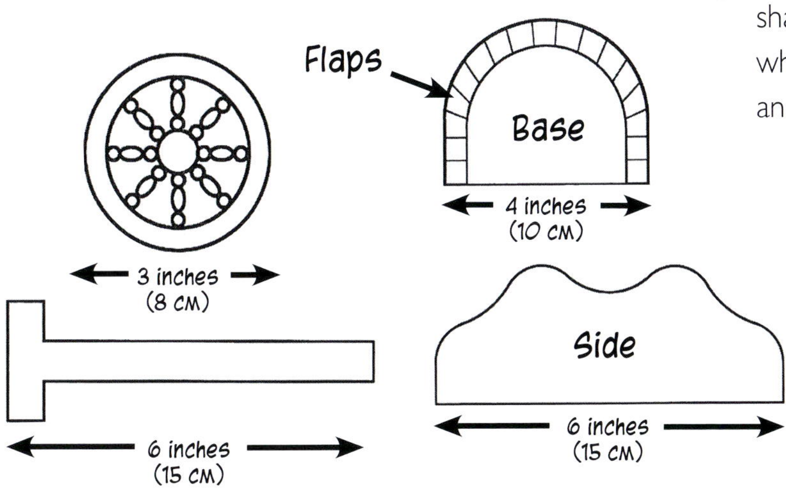

2. Snip around the edge of the base and fold up the flaps. Bend the side around the base and glue it onto the flaps.

3. Cut out two card circles 3 inches (8 cm) wide for the wheels and a T-shape for the chariot pole.

4. Either cut out spokes and hub shapes or draw them on. Stick a wheel on each side of the chariot and the T-shape onto the bottom.

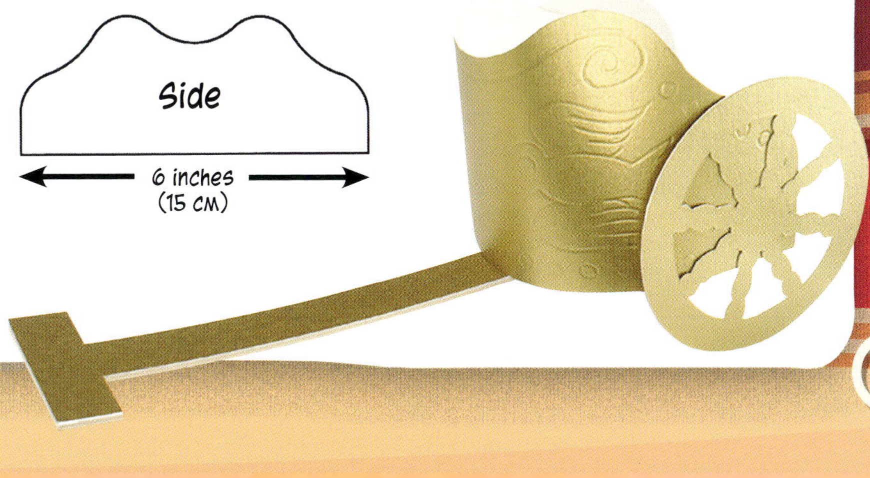

ROMAN BATHS

Public baths were places where people met and relaxed. They had central heating and five different kinds of pools. It only cost a penny to get in.

Instead of soap, oil was rubbed onto the skin and scraped off with a metal or bone **strigil**

Hot and cold

The Laconium was a hot room like a sauna with a tub of boiling water. The Caldarium was a hot room with a hot pool. The Tepidarium was a warm room with a warm pool. The Frigidarium had a large, cold pool. The Spa had mineral water to bathe in and drink for good health.

The water in the baths was heated by fires that warmed the air beneath the floor.

Beauty treatments

Massage, hairdressing, shaving, and other beauty treatments were offered at the baths. Enslaved people helped their masters and mistresses to dress and undress. The clothes were wrapped and held together with belts and pins.

This statue shows how brooches were used to hold folds of fabric together.

ACTIVITY

MAKE A DOLPHIN BROOCH

Ask an adult to help you with this activity

Dolphin shapes were often used in Roman jewelry.

You will need:

- **thick card stock**
- **colored shiny card stock**
- **scissors**
- **glue**
- **silver pen**
- **safety pin**
- **sticky tape**

1. Cut out the shape of a dolphin in thick card stock.

2. Decorate with shapes of colored shiny card stock. Outline the shapes with a silver pen.

3. Tape a safety pin on the back and ask an adult to help you pin it onto your clothes.

ROMAN TOWNS

In 79 CE, the volcano Mount Vesuvius in Italy erupted and buried the nearby town of Pompeii in ash. The city remained captured in a moment in time under the ash for 1,600 years until it was rediscovered. The remains show us what a Roman town was like.

Roman **aqueducts** can still be seen today. They carried fresh water into a town.

Layout

Roman towns were surrounded by walls. They often had temples, bathhouses, theaters, and an amphitheater. A typical town had two main roads running from north to south and from east to west, meeting at a square in the town center. Straight streets were lined with gutters that ran into underground sewers.

The ruins of Pompeii give us important clues about life in a Roman town.

Market goods

The **forum** was a busy market surrounded by shops, snack bars, and inns. In the market, you could buy large pottery jars called amphorae, which were used for storing food, and also bowls and plates.

Pottery was made in factories and used all over the Empire.

ACTIVITY

MAKE A SIMPLE COIL POT

You will need:
- **air-drying clay**
- **water**
- **modeling tool**

1. Roll out lots of long sausages of modeling clay.

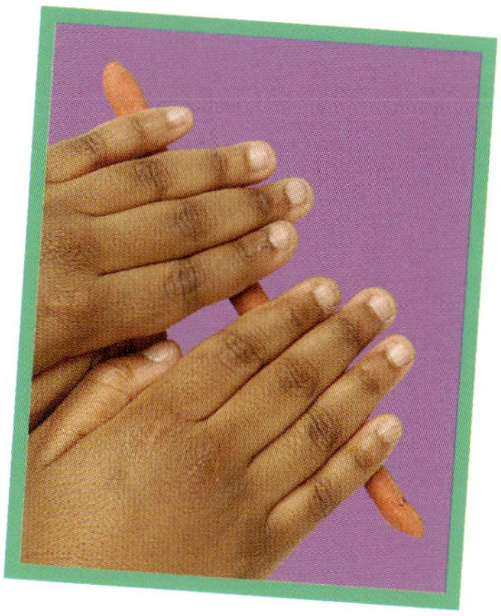

2. Coil one sausage around to make a flat circle for the base. Wet around the edge with water.

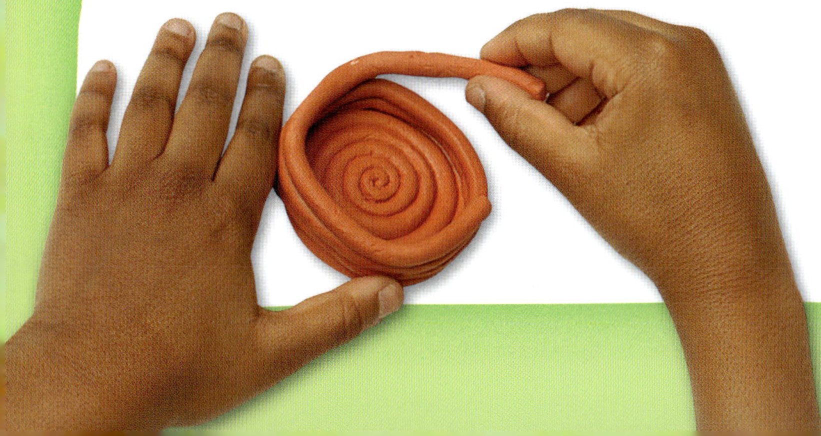

3. Build up the pot with coils of clay, wetting with water as you go to stick the layers of clay together.

4. Smooth the sides with a modeling tool and mark on a pattern. Leave to dry.

GODS AND MYTHS

The Romans worshipped many gods and goddesses. They believed the gods protected the Roman Empire. Towards the end of the Roman Empire, Christianity became the official religion.

Apollo was the god of sun, light, knowledge, music, and poetry.

Sacrifice

People brought animals to the temples as a **sacrifice** to please the gods. Priests killed the animals on an **altar** and special requests to the gods were made.

Jupiter, king of the gods, was the god of thunder and lightning. He carried a lightning bolt.

Ceres, goddess of the harvest, carried ears of corn.

Mars, the god of war, was said to be the father of Romulus and Remus.

Diana, goddess of the Moon and hunting, carried a bow and arrow.

Roman myths

The gods belonged to a family. Stories about them, called myths, explained what happened in the world. Neptune was the god of the sea and earthquakes. He rode a horse in the waves.

Neptune carried a large three-pronged spear called a trident.

ACTIVITY

MAKE A COLLAGE OF A GOD OR GODDESS

Choose a Roman god or goddess. Imagine what they would look like. This is Neptune.

You will need:

- **paper and pencil**
- **scrap material, colored paper, and yarn**
- **scissors**
- **glue**

1. Draw your god or goddess carrying their symbol.
2. Use pieces of material, colored paper, and yarn to give them clothes and hairstyles in the Roman style.

Glossary

altar

An altar is a table on which sacrifices to the gods were made.

amphitheater

An amphitheater is a round or oval-shaped building where Roman crowds watched gladiator fights.

aqueduct

An aqueduct is a bridge that carries water.

century

In Roman times, a century was a military group of about 100 soldiers, called centuries.

citizen

Roman citizens were men who were born in Rome, or who had fought for Rome. People in conquered lands could also become citizens.

conquer

To attack a place and take control over it. Romans conquered many countries, which then became part of the Roman Empire.

domus

Some wealthy Roman families had a town house called a domus.

empire

An empire is a group of countries ruled by an emperor or empress.

engineer

An engineer is a person who designs and builds roads and bridges.

forum

In Roman times, a public square or marketplace was called a forum.

gladiator

A gladiator was a fighter who entertained Roman crowds.

hippodrome

A hippodrome is an arena. It can have an oval-shaped track for racing.

insulae

Less wealthy Roman families often lived in apartment blocks called insulae.

knucklebones

Knucklebones was a game like modern jacks played with the small bones of animals.

legend

A legend is a traditional story that has been passed down through the ages.

legion

A legion is a large group of soldiers. In the Roman army, a legion had about 5,000 soldiers, called legionaries.

numeral

A numeral is a symbol that stands for a number.

papyrus

Papyrus is a type of paper made from reeds.

sacrifice

A sacrifice is an offering to the gods. Romans brought gifts of food or animals to the temple to be killed to please the gods.

senate

In Roman times, the senate was a group of people who formed part of the government.

senator

A senator was a member of the government who had been voted in by the people.

standard

A standard was a pole carried by a soldier that had the symbol of his legion on it.

strigil

A strigil was an instrument used by the Romans for scraping the skin after a bath.

toga

A toga was a loose piece of clothing worn in Ancient Rome.

villa

Some wealthy Roman families had a country house called a villa.

Quiz

1. **Who was the city of Rome named after?**

a) Romeo
b) Romola
c) Romulus
d) Remus

2. **Who was the first Roman emperor?**

a) Julius Caesar
b) Augustus Caesar
c) Claudius Caesar
d) Nero Caesar

3. **On average, how old was a Roman girl when she got married?**

a) 10 or 11
b) 13 or 14
c) 16 or 17
d) 18 or 19

4. **How long did a soldier serve in the Roman army?**

a) 5 years
b) 10 years
c) 20 years
d) 25 years

5. **Why did Roman actors wear masks?**

a) to hide their faces
b) so everyone could see their expressions
c) so men could act as women
d) so women could act as men

6. **How many different letters are used for Roman numerals?**

a) five
b) six
c) seven
d) eight

7. **Which of the following is NOT a type of Roman bath?**

a) Laconium
b) Caldarium
c) Tepidarium
d) Refridgarium

8. **Which volcano covered Pompeii in ash?**

a) Vesuvius
b) Etna
c) Krakatoa
d) Vulcano

9 **Who was the Roman god of the sun?**

a) Jupiter
b) Ceres
c) Apollo
d) Cupid

10 **What was the name of Neptune's spear?**

a) fork
b) trident
c) bayonet
d) harpoon

ANSWERS 1c, 2b, 3b, 4d, 5b, 6c, 7d, 8a, 9c, 10b

FURTHER INFORMATION

BOOKS

Finan, Catherine C. *Ancient Rome*. Minneapolis, MN: Bearport Publishing Company, 2022.

Levy, Janey. *The Feats of Ancient Rome*. Buffalo, NY: Gareth Stevens Publishing, 2022.

WEBSITES

Britannica Kids: Ancient Rome

https://kids.britannica.com/kids/article/ancient-Rome/353728

Check out maps, photographs, and more facts about how the ancient Romans lived!

National Geographic Kids: Ancient Rome

kids.nationalgeographic.com/history/article/ancient-rome

Learn more about how the ancient Romans lived.

Index